CHRISTMAS AROUND THE WORLD

FOR KIDS

Exploring Global Holiday Practices, Christmas Ornaments, Foods, Santa Representations, and Additional Celebrations

James Miller

Happy Holidays

to:

from:

Merry Christmas

AUSTRALIA

For Kids, Christmas in Australia feels different but also familiar. It takes place in summer. The sun shines bright. People gather at the beach. The smell of barbecues fills the air. You feel excitement in every corner.

The usual image of a cold Christmas doesn't work in Australia. The weather is hot. Snowmen don't last.

Food

You know how in cold places people have roast turkey for Christmas dinner? Some people in Australia still keep this tradition. Many love to take advantage of the summer weather. They prefer barbecues. They enjoy grilled shrimp. They roast chicken. They love their meat smoked and marinated.

Let's not leave out the salad. Almost every Christmas meal in Australia includes salad. This is because it's summer in December in Australia. Fresh summer fruits like mangoes and cherries find their way to the table too. Of course, a Christmas meal isn't complete without dessert. Some people love to devour a good Christmas pudding or fruitcake. But in Australia, people often enjoy the Pavlova. It's a fluffy, cloud-like dessert topped with whipped cream and fresh berries.

The figure of Santa Claus has a couple of modifications in Australia. Here, Santa changes his clothing. He wears shorts and flip-flops instead of a thick red suit. His mode of transport isn't reindeer. Kangaroos sometimes pull his sleigh. People often call them the "six white boomers." Sometimes, Santa arrives on a surfboard. The symbol of Santa is the same, though. He brings joy and gifts.

Christmas in Australia has wonderful decorations. The usual ornaments like lights, reefs, and Christmas trees are everywhere. The eucalyptus tree stands tall as the Christmas tree here. Instead of mistletoe, people hang bunches of "Christmas Bush," an Australian plant that flushed red during December. Some people decorate their homes with "Christmas Bell," a bell-shaped flower that blooms during Christmas time.

Songs fill the air in Australia during Christmas. Yes, there are the familiar tunes. You'll hear "Jingle Bells" or "Deck the Halls." People also sing special Australian carols. These tunes tell the story of Christmas in Australia. Their words speak about kangaroos, six white boomers, and Australia's natural beauty.

Marketplaces in Australia are festive during Christmas. Sydney's Fish Market opens for a 24-hour Seafood Marathon. This market has over 50 seafood sellers. This happens every year. Buyers have a range of excellent seafood to choose from.

Presents are important. Everyone loves receiving gifts. In Australia, gift-giving isn't different from any other part of the world. People exchange gifts with beloved family and friends. Some volunteer their time in charity as a way of gift-giving. Children in Australia write letters to Santa Claus asking for their presents. They leave out cookies and milk for Santa on the night before Christmas.

See? Every country celebrates Christmas in their special way, Australia included. The joy of Christmas is the same everywhere. That's what matters. Even if Santa rides kangaroos instead of reindeer in Australia.

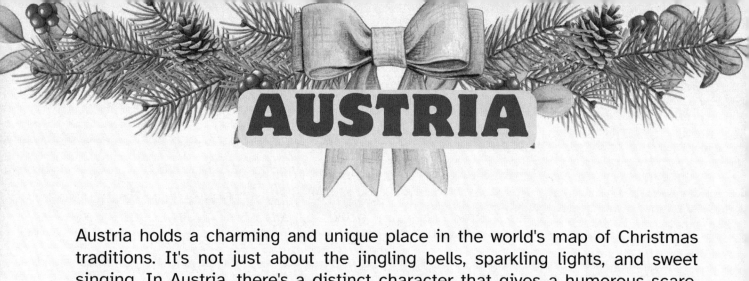

AUSTRIA

Austria holds a charming and unique place in the world's map of Christmas traditions. It's not just about the jingling bells, sparkling lights, and sweet singing. In Austria, there's a distinct character that gives a humorous scare. This character is known as Krampus, a creature that seems a little bit scary but shares an important lesson.

Krampus is a tall figure. He has horns and looks a little like a creature from a fairy tale. The story says that Krampus comes around every Christmas season. He's not here to give gifts. His job is to remind the kids to behave well and be good. While it can sound scary, it's all in good spirit and teaches children the importance of good behavior.

In Austria, Santa Claus has a different name. They call him "Nikolaus". Nikolaus doesn't come on Christmas day. He comes on the night of December 6. He brings small gifts, fruits, and chocolates. Parents leave the kids' shoes outside the door. Nikolaus puts the gifts inside the shoes.

When it comes to decorations, Austrians love to make their homes look happy and bright for Christmas. They decorate their homes with lights. They hang stars. They decorate a Christmas tree with ornaments, shiny baubles, and twinkling lights. Some people also put lanterns on their windows. The lanterns give a soft, comforting light. It makes the cold winter nights feel cozy.

The music and caroling traditions in Austria are very strong. People love to sing carols. They sing in their homes, in the streets, in the churches. Some traditional Austrian carols are "Silent Night" and "Oh You Joyful". In some parts of Austria, there's a special caroling tradition. A group of men dressed as shepherds and angels go from house to house. They sing carols and bring good wishes. This tradition is called "Glorifying".

Austria loves Christmas markets. The markets are full of small wooden stalls. They sell all kinds of things like crafts, toys, and food. The air is full of the smell of roasted chestnuts and hot mulled wine.

As for the gifts, children in Austria write letters to the Christ Child. They ask for the gifts they want. The gifts are usually opened on the night before Christmas.

Christmas season in Austria is full of cozy feelings, sweet smells, and joyful sounds. Even with the scary Krampus, the spirit of love, sharing, and good behavior is very strong.

BRAZIL

In the heart of South America, Christmas in Brazil stands out as a unique blend of different traditions. Papai Noel, the Brazilian version of Santa Claus, is a central figure in the holiday celebrations. Papai Noel, dressed in silk clothing due to Brazil's hot, summer Christmas, doesn't visit from the North Pole - instead, he comes from Greenland.

Gifts are delivered under the Christmas tree by Papai Noel on Christmas Eve. Brazilian kids, like other children around the globe, write letters to Papai Noel, sharing their wishes for Christmas. Some even hang socks near the window hoping that Papai Noel, following the old tradition, will swap them for presents.

In Brazil, it is customary to have a big family meal late on Christmas Eve and the early hours of Christmas Day. The feast, called Ceia de Natal, takes place after the Missa do Galo or the "Rooster's Mass" in Catholic Churches, so named because it can run until 1 A.M. The table is laden with a variety of foods: turkey, ham, colored rice, and wonderful fresh fruits like pineapple and mangoes, reflecting Brazil's rich cuisine. Brazilian Christmas food is colorful and appealing, a big part of the holiday festivities.

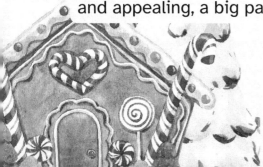

The drink of choice for many during these celebrations is a chilled glass of Rabanada. This is a Brazilian take on the French toast, a classic Christmas beverage that boasts the flavors of the season.

When it comes to decorations, Brazil truly sparkles. Christmas trees, both fake and real, are popular, and lights outline homes, buildings and line the city streets, lighting up the night with a festive glow. Churches and homes often display a "Presepio" or nativity scene with the models of Mary, Joseph, Jesus, and the three wise men in a stable. The scene often stays up until January 6th, a day known as Kings' Day that marks the visit of the Magi to baby Jesus.

Music and Caroling form a vital part of the celebration as well. People of all ages sing and dance to the tune of popular Christmas carols. Carolers visit neighborhood homes, spreading cheer and bringing the community together. Schools and local communities put on Plays depicting the holy nativity scene —a traditional way of welcoming the spirit of Christmas.

Alongside caroling, Brazil takes pride in its Christmas markets. From high-end shopping malls to local markets, many places host special Christmas fairs selling everything from unique artisan crafts to delicious culinary delights. Many city squares turn into a Christmas wonderland, with artisan crafts and food stalls, where people can buy traditional Christmas decorations, hand-made gifts, or even a sweet treat for the family Christmas table.

BRAZIL

As for gift-giving, it's not just Papai Noel who gets in on the fun. 'Amigo secreto', or 'secret friend', is a popular game in Brazil akin to 'secret Santa'. Much like the version known around the world, people draw names to determine who they will be buying a gift for, maintaining the secret until the gift exchange.

In summary, Christmas in Brazil is a heartfelt blend of universal Christmas traditions with a unique Brazilian flavor. From Papai Noel, late-night feasts, luminous decorations, and traditional carols to lively Christmas markets and thoughtful gifts, it's a warm and festive season under the Brazilian sun. Kids and adults alike find joy in the traditions, making merry and upholding the Christmas spirit.

CANADA

Canada's Christmas celebrations reflect the diversity and multiculturalism of the nation. Christmas traditions from a broad mix of cultures merge and create a unique Canadian holiday experience. On a chilly December day, Canadians from coast to coast start preparing for a festive season full of excitement and joy.

Santa Claus, known as "Père Noël" in French, is a beloved figure. He brings presents to the children. Like in many places, children write letters to Santa, sending their Christmas wishes. The Canadian postal service even has a special zip code for Santa: H0H 0H0. Each letter sent to this address receives a response.

Food and beverages play a prominent role at Christmas. A typical Canadian Christmas dinner includes roast turkey with stuffing, cranberries, and gravy. Other dishes often include roasted root vegetables, potatoes, and sweet items like butter tarts and mincemeat pie. Fudge and cookies are also common. Drinks often served during the season include hot chocolate, apple cider, and eggnog, a creamy drink made with eggs, milk, and sugar, often spiced with nutmeg and sometimes served with a dash of rum.

CANADA

As night falls, the country lights up. Canadians take festive decorations seriously, with many going all out to adorn their homes with outdoor lights. You'll see everything from simple, elegantly lit homes to extravagant light displays synchronized to Christmas carols. Some neighborhoods even hold friendly competition for the best light show.

Music adds to the holiday cheer. Caroling is a cherished tradition with popular songs like "Jingle Bells," "Silent Night," and "Deck the Halls" sung by many. Schools and churches often put on special Christmas concerts. Some cities host outdoor caroling events that draw crowds, creating a community celebration full of holiday spirit.

Christmas markets are also a huge draw. These markets, usually set up in the city center, are lively, cheerful places full of holiday spirit. It's here that you'll find everything from handmade crafts and decorations to locally made food and drink. You can shop for unique gifts, enjoy a hot beverage, and get into the Christmas spirit amidst the glow of festive lights.

CANADA

Gift-giving is a large part of the holiday tradition. Presents are usually exchanged on Christmas morning, with families gathering around the Christmas tree. Canadians often participate in "Secret Santa" gift exchanges, particularly in workplaces or amongst friends. For many, it's not just about the presents under the tree, but the time spent with loved ones.

When it comes to Christmas traditions, the Canadian way reflects the diversity of the nation. The customs and practices from different cultures blend together, creating a unique yuletide experience. From festive feasts and visiting Christmas markets to lighting displays and surrounding the Christmas tree for the morning's gift exchange, Canada's Christmas is a heartwarming, inclusive celebration. Be it a simple hot meal or a grand light display, every tradition brings people together, promoting unity and festivity. It is this togetherness, irrespective of the cold outside, that truly warms the holiday season in Canada.

CHINA

China, shaped by its blend of cultures and history, has a unique approach to Christmas. Since predominantly it's not a Christian country, the celebration of Christmas is not widespread. However, in major cities and among the younger generation, the holiday has gained popularity.

There isn't a specific Chinese version of Santa Claus, but an image of a stout, jolly gift-giver has made its way into the celebrations. In Mandarin, he is called 'Shengdan Laoren,' which means Old Christmas Man.

Traditionally, there's no specific Christmas meal in China. However, for those who do celebrate, a Western-style dinner with turkey and all the trimmings has become popular. Many restaurants and hotels that cater to foreigners or ex-pats often serve a Christmas dinner. In addition to this, apples are often given as gifts on Christmas Eve, because in Mandarin, Christmas Eve is 'Ping'an Ye,' which sounds like the word for apple. These apples are often wrapped in colored paper and given as tokens of good luck.

Cities like Beijing, Shanghai, and Guangzhou light up during Christmas. Sparkling lights and decorations adorn buildings and streets, creating a festive atmosphere. Western-style Christmas trees pop up in shopping malls and public spaces, adorned with lights and ornaments. Theme parks go the extra mile, hosting special Christmas-themed events with shows and displays that light up the chilly night.

CHINA

Music casts a cheerful spell on the celebrations. English Christmas carols can be heard in shopping malls and other public places while international schools might put on Christmas concerts. Among those who celebrate Christmas, it's common to have Christmas parties with music and gift exchanges.

Christmas markets are held in some of China's biggest cities. These markets, often organized by foreign communities, bring a touch of Western Christmas to China. Stalls at these markets sell a variety of goods, from Christmas decorations and handmade crafts to foreign food and drink.

When it comes to gift-giving, this is mostly done among close friends and loved ones. In China, the act of giving gifts is a reflection of respect and friendship. For those who celebrate Christmas, traditional Western gifts like toys, candies, and accessories are common. However, giving apples on Christmas Eve has become a unique practice in China.

While Christmas isn't a public holiday in China, its spirit is alive in the country's major cities. For the Chinese who celebrate, it's often less about tradition and more about having a good time. It's a season for fun decorations, Western style-festivals, delicious food, and spending time with loved ones. The way Christmas is celebrated in China reflects the nation's ability to adapt foreign customs and add a unique Chinese touch to them. Despite the cold winter weather, Christmas brings a certain warmth to the cities for both locals and tourists alike.

COLOMBIA

Colombia is a South American country known for its vibrant culture and traditions. It has a unique way of marking the start of the Christmas season. A very special event known as 'Little Candles' Day' sets it apart from many other nations. This day is recognized on the 7th of December. It gives a unique start to the holiday season. As twilight sets in, families, neighbors, and communities come together. They light candles and paper lanterns. This event fills the streets, sidewalks, balconies, porches, and driveways with a beautiful, soulful light. It creates a sense of unity, warmth, and anticipation for the joyous celebration to come.

This tradition is a visual treat. It also serves to honor the Virgin Mary and the Immaculate Conception. It brings communities together in a shared luminance. Groups and families gather around their displays. They socialize, sharing food and drinks along with laughter and stories.

Colombia offers unique foods and beverages during Christmas. It is known for dishes like natilla and buñuelos. Natilla is a custard-like dessert. Buñuelos are cheesy fritters. They are the favorite treats during Christmas celebrations. Beverages like 'chorizo' punch and 'aguapanela' with cheese are also popular.

COLOMBIA

Colombian Christmas traditions vary from town to town. The Novena de Aguinaldos is a typically common ritual. This nine-day period leading up to Christmas Day involves prayer, singing, and feasting. Families and friends rotate hosting it. This event brings people together in a spiritual, felicitous union.

In Colombia, Santa Claus is known as 'El Niño Jesus'. He brings gifts for children. This figure is not the traditional bearded man we know in red suit. Instead, the Colombian Santa is believed to be the Christ child himself. He brings both gifts and blessings to the home.

Christmas decorations in Colombia are both vibrant and symbolic. The light from 'Little Candles' Day' continues to illuminate homes. It extends with Christmas lights and ornate nativity scenes. Christmas trees and 'pesebres' or nativity scenes are very important in Colombia. The central figure of the child Jesus holds a place of honor.

Christmas music plays a vital role in the Colombian Yuletide. Caroling is popular. Songs like 'El Niño del Tambor' and 'Los Peces en el Río' echo through the streets. They reflect the joy and spirit of the occasion.

Colombian towns and cities host 'Ferias' or Fair events. They offer a blend of religious and festive activities. Colorful parades, music concerts, and fireworks provide entertainment for all. It draws locals and tourists alike.

COLOMBIA

Gift-giving customs in Colombia often involve 'El Niño Jesus' leaving gifts for children to find on Christmas day. The joy of this tradition reflects the heart of Colombian Christmas. It's the sense of family, faith, and community. It's beautifully symbolized by the millions of lights that glow on 'Little Candles' Day'.

CZECH REPUBLIC

In the heart of Europe lies the Czech Republic. It is a nation that values its unique Christmas customs. One such tradition involves an extra place setting at the Christmas dinner table. It is a symbolic gesture meant for an unexpected guest, or as locals believe, for the baby Jesus.

When it comes to the traditional Christmas food, Czechs enjoy a hearty feast. The meal often involves fish soup followed by fried carp and potato salad. Carp is a significant choice, with families often buying the fish live and keeping it in the bathtub before they prepare it for the meal. Christmas desserts include 'Vanocka'. It's a sweet bread decorated with almonds and raisins.

Czech Christmas traditions are numerous. The Advent period before Christmas is filled with preparations. People bake cookies, decorate their homes and prepare the Christmas feast. Czechs also celebrate Saint Nicholas Day. On this eve, men dress as devils, angels, and St. Nicholas. They visit homes, testing if the children have been good during the past year.

In the Czech Republic, Santa Claus is replaced by 'Jezisek' or baby Jesus. While he shares Santa's gift-giving role, Jezisek lacks the older man's iconic look. He is depicted as a small, Christ-like figure devoid of specific physical attributes. He doesn't come down the chimney. Instead, the window is left ajar for Jezisek to deliver his gifts.

CZECH REPUBLIC

Christmas decorations in the Czech Republic are often handmade, adding a personal touch to the season. Fragrant gingerbread cookies, intricately painted eggs, and straw decorations are common. Christmas trees are also popular and are often decorated with traditional Czech Christmas ornaments.

Music plays a significant role in Czech Christmas celebrations. Caroling is a common practice, with many Czechs taking part in it. Familiar carols like 'Nesem vam noviny' ('We Bring You News') fill the air during the holiday season.

The Czech Republic showcases an array of Christmas markets. One of the most spectacular is the Prague Christmas Market. It's hailed for its beautiful setting and festive atmosphere. Czech Christmas markets sell everything from handmade toys to aromatic Czech Christmas cookies.

Gift-giving in the Czech Republic happens on Christmas Eve, delivered by Jezisek. The hidden ideology behind the gifts is the spreading of happiness and cheer. The exchange of presents occurs under the glow of the Christmas tree after dinner is had and carols are sung. The glow in the children's eyes while opening presents reflects the joy and cheer of the season.

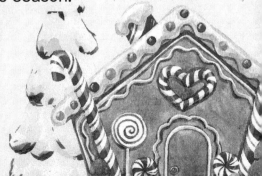

CZECH REPUBLIC

The Czech Republic's Christmas is a blend of spiritual devotion and centuries-old folklore. The extra place setting, the special feast, and the visit from Jezisek — all these elements combine to create a warm, inviting celebration that honours past traditions. It highlights the importance of love, family, and charity during the holiday season. This way, it amicably welcomes everyone into the fold of its charming Yuletide spirit.

DENMARK

In the cold climes of Northern Europe, Denmark holds the warmth of Christmas close to its heart. Christmas in Denmark comes with its joyous spirit and a host of unique traditions. A lovable figure known as Julemanden or 'Christmas Man' visits on Christmas Eve, bearing gifts and accompanied by his mischievous elves, known as 'Nisser'.

Danish Christmas foods are a feast of delightful flavors. The Christmas Eve dinner often includes roast duck or goose, boiled potatoes, and plenty of gravy, known as 'Brun Sauce'. Dessert usually features 'Risalamande'. It is a cold rice pudding with cherry sauce. The Danes love to drink 'Gløgg', a delightful Danish Christmas mulled wine during such occasions.

Christmas traditions in Denmark zone in on the coziness of the season. The term for this in Danish is 'hygge'. The start of Christmas festivities is symbolized by the lighting of the Advent wreath. Four Sundays before Christmas, a candle is lit. Then every subsequent Sunday, another candle joins it until all four candles are lit. Another essential Danish tradition is 'Julefrokost', or 'Christmas lunch', featuring a wide spread of Danish favorites.

DENMARK

Danish people welcome Julemanden or 'Christmas Man', their unique version of Santa Claus, with excitement. Julemanden comes from Greenland. He is aided by cheerful yet cheeky little elves known as 'Nisser'. The Nisser live in attics or barns and are known to play tricks on people if not kept in good spirits with a bowl of rice pudding, a popular Christmas dessert.

Christmas decorations in Denmark are simple yet filled with lots of 'hygge'. Homemade heart and star-shaped Christmas ornaments are popular. They use everything from paper to apple slices for decorations. The centerpiece of a Danish Christmas home is the Christmas tree adorned with lights, Danish flags, homemade decorations, and a star to top it off.

Christmas music fills every corner of Denmark during the holiday season. Carol singing in Danish is known as 'Syng jule ind'. Carolers walk from house to house, spreading cheer through song. Some of the favorite Danish Christmas carols include 'Jul, det' cool' and 'Jingle Bells'.

Denmark is famous for its Christmas markets. The most beautiful one can be found in Copenhagen in the Tivoli Gardens. It's a winter wonderland, filled with twinkling light displays, charming wooden huts selling Danish crafts and delicacies, and even an ice-skating rink. The atmosphere is full of Christmas spirit.

DENMARK

Gift-giving is an anticipated tradition. On Christmas Eve, after the meal, everyone gathers around the Christmas tree. They hold hands and move around the tree singing carols. Following this, gifts from Julemanden, placed under the Christmas tree, are opened.

From the hearty Christmas meals, cozy decorations, the sight of Julemanden and his elfin assistants, to the grand festival markets, Christmas in Denmark is indeed a magical experience. It represents the Danish sense of 'hygge' – warmth, coziness, and a sense of well-being. It's Denmark's way of casting out the darkness of winter and filling homes and hearts with Christmas joy.

EGYPT

Egypt, a land rich in history and culture, is known for the unique way its Coptic Christian community celebrates Christmas. The celebration takes place on January 7th, marked by special liturgies and fasts. Unlike the way many other countries celebrate the Christian holiday, Egypt's Coptic Christians have some unique customs tied to their country's history and culture.

Traditional food and beverages are integral parts of festivities. Fasting plays a crucial role in these Christmas celebrations. For 43 days before Christmas, referred to as the Holy Nativity Fast, people follow a vegan diet. No animal products are consumed. Coptic Christians break this fast after the midnight mass service on Christmas day. The meal that follows is often composed of meat, eggs, butter, and cheese, foods abstained from during fasting. A popular dish during this time is "fata", a stew with bread, rice, garlic, and boiled meat.

One of the customs Coptic Christians follow is attending special liturgies. The liturgy usually starts at 10:30 PM and goes on until past midnight. It may extend up to 4:00 AM. During these hours, people attend the Church services where they pray, sing hymns, and listen to the sermon. The service ends with the congregation receiving Holy Communion.

EGYPT

Coptic Christians do not have a Santa Claus per se, but children still receive gifts. Instead of a jolly man in a red suit, these presents are often attributed to the Baby Jesus. Presents are given to children after the Christmas feast, marking the end of the long fast and the joyous occasion.

In terms of decorations for Christmas, Coptic Christians don't typically decorate a tree or put up stockings. The churches, however, are decorated beautifully with lights. Christian households also use a Coptic icon in their home during the Advent season. This iconography, depicting various scenes from the Bible, adds a religious touch to their decorations.

Music is also an essential part of Coptic Christian celebrations. Deacons in the church wear special tunics and sing hymns in ancient Egyptian language, which is known as the Coptic language. This language has been preserved and used exclusively in their Christian liturgy. Some of these songs are specific to the Nativity period and Christmas feast.

In cities like Cairo and Alexandria, there are Christmas markets where people can buy decorations, gifts, and Coptic icons. They sell crosses, pictures of saints, and other religious items. These markets add a festive ambiance to the streets of Egypt.

EGYPT

Gifts are an integral part of Christmas celebrations everywhere, and Coptic Christians are no different. But in the Coptic tradition, it's the Baby Jesus who gives gifts to children, not Santa. Parents usually hide the presents and tell their children that the angel of the Baby Jesus had come overnight and left the presents for them.

Egypt's Coptic Christian Christmas observance is both solemn and joyful. The observance is a unique fusion of traditional Christian practices and ancient Egyptian culture which has been carried on for centuries. It provides valuable insight into how varied, rich, and deep our global cultural practices can be. From the delicious traditional foods that break the long fast to the important religious liturgies, the tradition of Christmas in Egypt is truly one of a kind and a fascinating component of Egypt's vibrant culture.

ETHIOPIA

In Ethiopia, Christmas is known as "Ganna" and is celebrated on January 7th. This holiday stands out for many reasons, particularly because of its unique games and traditional foods that are unlike any other region.

Christmas food in Ethiopia is a special affair. While many are enjoying rich and festive cuisine, Ethiopian Orthodox Christians end a 40-day fast on Ganna called the "fast of the prophets". The Christmas day feast that breaks this fast typically includes Doro Wat. This is a spicy chicken stew laced with Berbere spice and served with Injera, a sourdough flatbread. Other dishes such as Kitfo, a meat dish, Tibs, a lamb dish, and traditional honey wine accompany the main course.

The traditions and rituals surrounding Ganna are distinctive. It all starts with a religious service that commences early in the morning. Church-goers wear a traditional white garment known as a Shamma. The churches, designed in a circular shape, fill with worshipers. The men and boys sit separately from the women and girls. The center of the church is saved for the choir, who sing hymns and dance. Priests don robes in the colors of the Ethiopian flag and carry ornately covered Bibles and crosses.

No Santa Claus figure exists in Ethiopian Christmas tradition. Instead, the focus is on the religious celebration of Christ's birth. Gifts are not a common part of the celebration either. The emphasis is on the spiritual rather than the material.

Decorations, too, are simple. Homes aren't decked out with bright symbols of the season like in other cultures. The churches, however, are often vibrantly decorated with lights. Many Ethiopian Orthodox Christians carry a candle home from the Christmas service and use it to light a little bonfire at their house.

Music plays a big part in the Ganna celebrations. The church service is accompanied by traditional music played on unique instruments. The "Mekdes" is a drum used by priests, while the congregation often accompanies hymns with "Sistrum", a type of rattle, and "Kerar", a stringed instrument. People clap rhythmically to the chants, adding to the joyful music of the service.

There aren't any grand Christmas markets in Ethiopia. But around the church areas, people sell little religious souvenirs or simple refreshments for the church-goers.

Gift-giving is not a focus of Ethiopian Ganna. The holiday centers more on religious observance, family, and community. However, baby Jesus features prominently in the Ganna story. Children often reenact the nativity scene with dolls.

Ganna stands out with the game from which the Christmas day takes its name. Ganna is a game played with sticks and wooden balls, not unlike hockey. Later in the holiday season, on January 19th, Ethiopians celebrate Timkat, the Epiphany, marking Jesus's baptism. The holy Tabot, a model of the Ark of the Covenant, is paraded around in a procession with singing, dancing, and ceremony.

You'll find that Ethiopian Ganna is not about materialistic festivities. It's about faith, worship, and community. The celebration of Ganna showcases the richness of cultural diversity, where something as universally recognized as Christmas can take on a unique rhythm that respectfully pays homage to its local heritage and practices. Ethiopia's Christmas celebration is a wonderful reflection of the country's deep faith and vibrant culture.

FINLAND

In Finland, Christmas holds a magical charm. It's believed that Santa Claus himself, known as Joulupukki, comes from Lapland, an area in northern Finland. This adds an extra dose of joy to the holiday season for both children and adults alike. Finnish yuletide traditions have a unique blend of old and new, from traditional foods to festive rituals.

Food is a cornerstone of Finnish Christmas celebrations. Christmas Eve's main meal typically includes a variety of dishes such as pickled herring, beetroot salad, and a casserole made from carrots, potatoes, or swede. Finns enjoy glazed ham with mustard as the centerpiece of their Christmas dinner, teamed with mulled wine, also known as warming Glögi, spiced with cloves and cinnamon and often served with raisins and almonds.

Traditions and rituals differ slightly compared to typical western celebrations. Unlike places that celebrate on the morning of December 25, Finnish Christmas festivities kick off on Christmas Eve. Many Finns visit cemeteries to remember lost loved ones, then enjoy a sauna before evening's festive feast. After eating, children eagerly await Joulupukki.

FINLAND

There are different takes on Santa Claus worldwide. In Finland, Santa is known as Joulupukki, translating to "Yule Goat". Unlike the Santa Claus who is known to sneak down chimneys during the wee hours of Christmas morning, Joulupukki often visits homes personally, knocking on the door right after Christmas dinner.

Decorations for Christmas in Finland often involve natural elements. Instead of artificial lights and glitz, Finns prefer decorating with candles, evergreens, and simple ornaments. Many Finnish homes display Christmas stars in their windows, emitting a warm, welcoming glow against the snowy winterscape.

Song is deeply embedded in Finnish Christmas. Traditional Christmas carols ring out across the country during the holiday season. Some favorite melodies include "Sylvian Joululaulu" and "Jouluyö, Juhlayö" - the Finnish version of "Silent Night".

Finland becomes a winter wonderland during Christmas, with markets sprung up across cities and towns. The Christmas market in Helsinki, known as Tuomaan Markkinat, is the largest and most festive in the country. With hundreds of stalls selling crafts, food, and other Christmas goods, it truly captures the spirit of the season.

FINLAND

Gift-giving plays a part in Finnish Christmas, much like in other cultures. But instead of being delivered by a stealthy Santa under the cloak of darkness, gifts are often given out by Joulupukki himself. This moment can be the highlight of Christmas for many Finnish children, as Joulupukki sometimes interacts with them, asking if they've been good during the year.

Christmas in Finland is a time of warmth amidst the cold, a time to slow down, enjoy festive food and drink, and spend time with loved ones. The charm of Finland's landscape, coupled with their unique yuletide traditions, makes Finnish Christmas both enchanting and distinct. From the hearty fare at Christmas markets to the anticipation of a visit from Joulupukki, the Finnish way of celebrating Christmas captures the true spirit of the holiday in its joyful, loving atmosphere.

FRANCE

France has a reputation for being a country of traditions and celebrations. Of these, there are two that stand out when Christmas season rolls around - The Feast of St. Nicholas on December 6th, and Réveillon, a late-night feast on Christmas Eve. These events come steeped in history. They serve as a showcase of local traditions and customs and offer a unique look into the people who call this country their home.

The Feast of St. Nicholas has been a part of French traditions for ages. On this day, children throughout the country eagerly await the arrival of St. Nicholas. It is said that on the eve of December 6, children place their shoes in front of the fireplace. If kids have been good, they would wake up the next morning to find small treats and gifts in their shoes, a tradition attributed to St. Nicholas himself. This includes items such as candies, fruits, and small toys.

In contrast to the wholesome joyfulness of The Feast of St. Nicholas, there also exists a darker character, Le Père Fouettard. While St. Nicholas rewards good children, Le Père Fouettard is there to punish those who have misbehaved. It serves as a reminder that this season is not only about celebration but also about reinvigorating the sense of right and wrong.

FRANCE

After the Feast of St. Nicholas, preparations for Réveillon begin. This is a major event that typically gathers the entire family for a feast, a means to share food and love at the end of the year. The night is blessed with dishes that include seafood, such as oysters and crab, poultry such as turkey, and the famous foie gras. It is a feast of epic proportions, matched only by the joy and laughter that echo through the home.

In France, Santa Claus takes the form of Père Noël. Dressed in red and white, he also rewards well-behaved children with gifts. But instead of stockings, French children hang their shoes near the chimney for Père Noël to fill with gifts.

Decorations play a big part during Christmas in France. Houses are adorned with nativity scenes, which include little clay figures called "santons". The most common symbol, the Christmas tree or "sapin de noël", is decorated with tinsel, lights, and colorful ornaments.

While the streets of France are filled with the melodious tunes of carolers, the highlight for many is the Christmas markets. They bring a festive ambience with food and beverage stalls, ice rinks, and various entertaining events. It is a place where children can buy small presents for their families, and the air is filled with the fragrance of mulled wine and roasting chestnuts.

FRANCE

On Christmas day, families exchange gifts. It is a day celebrated with love, warmth and happiness. So, for those who want to experience the magic of Christmas, France, with its blend of historic tradition and holiday cheer, is the perfect place. The Feast of St. Nicholas and Réveillon will surely leave delicious memories, warm hearts, and a bright start for the coming year.

GERMANY

The spirit of Christmas shines bright in Germany, a country renowned for its festive markets and the beloved tradition of the Advent wreath. As soon as the holiday season begins, a sense of joy and anticipation fills the air.

Germany has a host of traditional Christmas foods and beverages enjoyed by many. Stollen, a delicacy akin to fruitcake, permeates through homes and bakeries. This bread-like cake, filled with dried fruits, nuts, and spices, generously dusted with icing sugar, has been a part of the German Christmas tradition for centuries. Alongside stollen, there are the famous Lebkuchen, German gingerbread cookies, a taste that is closely associated with the festive season. A sip of Glühwein (mulled wine), usually accompanied by a dash of rum or brandy, is another Christmastime favorite.

Also, much rooted in German tradition is the Advent wreath. Four candles adorn these wreaths, typically made of fir tree branches, pine cones, berries, and ribbons. Starting from the first Sunday of Advent, people light one candle each week, leading up to Christmas. This symbolizes the passing of the four weeks of Advent in anticipation of Christmas.

Santa Claus or Weihnachtsmann, as the Germans call him, makes a special appearance on Christmas Eve. Children often leave letters for Weihnachtsmann on their windowsills, filled with holiday wishes and promises of good behavior. As per the folklore, He delivers gifts and sweets to the good children, while the naughty ones are visited by the scary creature called Krampus.

GERMANY

The magic of Christmas carols cannot be ignored in Germany. Known as Weihnachtslieder, these carols are traditionally sung on Christmas Eve. Iconic carols like "Silent Night" and "O Tannenbaum" have their origins in Germany.

The Christmas markets, or Weihnachtsmarkt, however, remain the highlight of the season in Germany. Lined with beautifully decorated stalls that sell decorations, crafts, toys, and food, these markets are a big draw for locals and tourists alike. Nothing beats the feeling of walking around a German Christmas market, with a cup of hot Glühwein in hand, taking in the illuminating lights, watching people ice-skating, and listening to the local choir singing carols.

Gift-giving in Germany takes place on Christmas Eve. Children secretly hang their boot or the stocking by the fireplace, hoping Weihnachtsmann will leave a present while they sleep. This ritual is accompanied by family gatherings where everyone exchanges gifts and enjoys a hearty meal.

In essence, the celebration of Christmas in Germany is a rich blend of food, music, decorations, and joyful festivities. The tradition of the Christmas markets and the Advent wreath is evidence of how deeply ingrained and valued these customs are in German culture. It truly offers a magical Christmas experience that creates memories of a lifetime.

GREECE

Christmas in Greece is a time for family, faith, and festivity. It is known for two distinctive customs - decorating boats instead of trees and venerating St. Nicholas, the protector of sailors.

Greek Christmas food traditions are abundant and varied. Melt-in-the-mouth cookies known as kourabiedes and melomakarona, honey cookies heavily spiced with cinnamon and clove, are beloved by all. A sweet bread named Christopsomo, or "Christ's Bread," is also baked and eaten on Christmas Day. It's usually round and adorned with a cross. A popular festive drink is Christougenniatiko, a spiced alcoholic beverage.

Greeks have a slightly different take on their decorations. Instead of decorating trees as many other countries do, they take great pride in decorating boats. This stems from the country's deep history and connection with the sea. It is also a sign of respect for those who risk their lives in the sea, such as sailors and fishermen. Today, this tradition still stands and it's not uncommon to see houses with lit up model boats by the window.

St. Nicholas is venerated in Greece. Known as the protector of sailors, he holds a special place in the hearts of Greeks. His feast day on December 6th often marks the beginning of the holiday season. Though not the traditional Santa Claus, St. Nicholas is often associated with gift-giving and generosity.

GREECE

In Greece, they also celebrate with Kallikantzaroi, a kind of goblin or sprite. Greek children know that these naughty goblins can cause mischief around the house during the 12 days of Christmas. To prevent this, they keep the fire burning throughout this period.

Christmas caroling, or kalanda, is popular with Greek children. They visit homes in their neighborhood, singing carols and playing triangles or drums. In return, they receive treats such as sweets, dried fruits, and small amounts of money.

The streets of Greece become alive with Christmas markets. These are much smaller than their European counterparts but are no less enchanting. They offer a variety of foods, goods, and treats. Stalls selling roasted chestnuts and loukoumades - sweet honey-soaked doughnuts, fill the air with tempting aromas.

Gift-giving in Greece traditionally happens on St. Basil's Day on January 1st, rather than Christmas. St. Basil, similar to St. Nicholas, is known for his generosity and care for the poor. He is thus the Greek equivalent of Santa Claus. On this day, children are given gifts, continuing the spirit of love and goodwill.

Thus, the celebration of Christmas in Greece is a beautiful fusion of customs, faith, and festivity. The tradition of decorating boats and honoring St. Nicholas emphasizes their respect for the sea and those who navigate it. This, coupled with the pleasures of the holiday season, makes a Greek Christmas a truly unique experience.

GREENLAND

Greenland celebrates Christmas in a distinct way. It embraces a blend of its native customs and Christian traditions. Mattak, a special delicacy of whale skin, becomes a unique part of the Christmas feast. Men serving women at the feast is another unique tradition upheld with great respect.

The land becomes a snow-filled paradise during Christmas. The traditional houses, covered in thick blankets of snow, shine under the soft glow of Christmas lights. The homes provide warmth against the biting cold, decorated with bright baubles, dazzling lights, holly, and candles.

The making of mattak, a prized delicacy, becomes a group activity. Whole communities come together to hunt the whale, cut the mattak, and share the bounty. This delicacy is eaten raw with a touch of salt.

By tradition, the Christmas feast is prepared and arranged by the men. On the day of the feast, the men serve hot and spicy dishes and drinks. They play the role of hosts, while the women enjoy their meal as esteemed guests.

The Greenlanders respect and learn from their surroundings. An important part of their Christmas celebrations is a visit by Santa Claus. In Greenland, Santa Claus arrives in a dogsled, reflecting the Inuit mode of transport. Children leave their shoes out in the hope that Santa will fill them with gifts and treats.

>>> WHILE MAE <<<

GREENLAND

Christmas music fills the icy air of Greenland during the holiday season. Groups of carolers roam the snow-covered streets during the days leading up to Christmas. They bring joy to their neighbors, singing timeless carols with soft, harmonious voices.

Handicraft markets abound during the Christmas season. Greenlands celebrate the holiday by sharing homemade crafts and goods. Locally made Christmas ornaments, candles, and knitted items often fill the markets. These festive markets are a platform for the local artisans to share their trades and crafts.

Gift-giving is a cherished custom in Greenland at Christmastime. Gifts are carefully chosen, wrapped, and placed under the Christmas tree. The joy of gift-opening is celebrated on Christmas morning. This exchange highlights togetherness, symbolizing respect and good wishes for one another.

Greenland's unique Christmas traditions embody the country's lifestyle, reflecting a harmony between the people and nature. The foods, including mattak, the men serving women at feasts, and the unique appearance of Santa Claus, all contribute to the joy and warmth of this special time of year.

GUATEMALA

In Guatemala, Christmas is a colorful, lively event. The celebrations start early with the Burning of the Devil. On December 7th, people take to the streets to burn trash and effigies. This ritual marks the start of the holiday season. It symbolizes cleaning away evil spirits and making way for the joyous Christmas celebrations.

Traditional Christmas foods are a highlight in Guatemala. The main dishes include tamales, a type of filled corn dough wrap, and ponche, a warm fruit punch often enjoyed on Christmas Eve. These foods, filled with unique flavors and spices, bring warmth to the chilly December nights.

Santa Claus, known as El Niño Dios, comes on Christmas Eve to leave presents near the nativity scene. This belief instills a sense of awe and excitement in children. They eagerly wait for their gifts.

Guatemalan Christmas decorations are filled with cheerful colors. The nativity scene, locally known as nacimiento, is a key symbol. Families set up elaborate nativity scenes, often spending days to perfect it. Along with the nativity scenes, colorful paper lanterns, called farolitos, are lit across towns and villages. Their soft glow fills the Christmas night with a serene beauty.

Caroling is a significant part of Guatemalan Christmas traditions. These peaceful melodies echo through the crisp winter nights. Families and friends sing traditional carols together, lighting up homes with their harmonies.

GUATEMALA

Guatemala hosts festive markets during Christmas. The markets sell all sorts of holiday goods, from food to crafts. Artisans showcase their skills at these markets, selling handcrafted items and unique gifts.

Gift-giving is an important part of the Guatemalan Christmas traditions. On Christmas Eve, family members exchange carefully wrapped gifts. The joy of opening these presents together creates lasting memories.

The traditions in Guatemala, from the Burning of the Devil to the colorful decorations, the festive music, and the warm family gatherings, all echo the cheerful spirit of Christmas. These customs, passed down through generations, keep the spirit of Christmas alive in the hearts of Guatemalans.

In conclusion, what makes Christmas in Guatemala unique and special is not the grandeur or the glamour, but the sentiment of familial love and warmth suffused into every tradition. It's a celebration of togetherness, and an invitation to share the warmth in the biting cold of December.

ICELAND

Iceland's Christmas celebration is marked by its folklore that features the Yule Lads. These thirteen mischievous fellows visit children during the 13 days leading up to Christmas. Each night, one Yule Lad visits homes, leaving small gifts in children's shoes or playfully causing mayhem.

Traditional Icelandic Christmas food is a beguiling blend of unique flavors. The Christmas buffet often showcases dishes like smoked lamb, and a drink, known as Malt og Appelsín, is a popular holiday beverage. It's a blend of malt and orange soda, lending a sweet note to the festive feast.

Santa Claus has a special place in Icelandic Christmas traditions. Unlike the single jolly figure known to the rest of the world, Iceland children anticipate the visit of not one but the thirteen Yule Lads. In place of a bag of toys, they bring a sense of delight with their amusing antics.

In Iceland, Christmas decorations stand out for their simplicity and elegance. Traditional decorations feature a lot of natural elements, like sprigs of evergreen plants, pine cones, and branches of rowan. Lights twinkle in almost every window, brightening the long winter nights.

Music flows into every corner of Iceland during Christmas. This country holds a deep affection for Christmas carols or Yule songs. Groups of carolers bring in the Yuletide spirit, their joyful tunes resonating across the icy landscapes.

ICELAND

Festive markets illuminate the December darkness in Iceland. Handcrafted gifts, seasonal treats, and traditional decorations are displayed under the tented booths. The aroma of roasting almonds, sizzling sausages, and spiced wine wafts across these Christmas markets.

Gift-giving in Iceland is not just a Christmas Day event. The exchange of gifts takes place over several days, thanks to the Yule Lads. Each night, children leave a shoe at their window, hoping to wake up to a small present left by the visiting Yule Lad.

Christmas in Iceland is a blend of time-honored traditions and an embrace of the natural landscape. The tradition of the Yule Lads adds a unique touch, creating a sense of anticipation and delight among children. The spirit of Christmas blooms amidst the icy beauty of Iceland. The warmth of love, the joy of food, the charm of music, and the pleasure of gifts come together to create a magical Christmas experience.

INDIA

In India, Christmas is celebrated with vibrant colors, fragrant food, and joyous music. India's diverse cultures have influenced the celebration of Christmas here. In some parts of India, people decorate banana or mango trees instead of the traditional Christmas tree, making each celebration unique.

Food plays an integral part in an Indian Christmas. Traditional foods include sweets like kulkuls, rose cookies, and Christmas pudding. Special beverages like wine brewed from rice or other grain add warmth to the meals.

The Indian version of Santa Claus, known as Christmas Baba, brings gifts to kids. Indian homes often have their doors open on Christmas Eve to welcome Christmas Baba, creating a sense of eagerness and enchantment among children.

Christmas decorations in India are brightly colorful. Many Indians decorate banana or mango trees, and the houses are illuminated with clay lamps. Star-shaped lanterns, symbolizing the Star of Bethlehem, adorn rooftops and door entrances.

INDIA

The beauty of Indian Christmas traditions and rituals extends to music and singing as well. Indo-western carols or songs retain the essence of Christ's birth yet carry a distinctive Indian beat. People sing these with joyful enthusiasm, infusing Christmas spirit into every corner.

Christmas markets, or fairs, add to the festive vibe in India. Rows of stalls display an array of products like handcrafted items, clothes, jewelry, and mouth-watering food. These markets are bustling with locals and tourists alike, looking for the perfect Christmas trinkets.

Gift-giving is an exciting part of an Indian Christmas. In the weeks leading up to Christmas, families shop for presents that are usually opened on Christmas morning. The process of exchanging gifts is a time for families to gather, share love and create unforgettable memories.

In summary, Indian Christmas is a unique blend of traditions and unity. The country's diverse cultures converge to create a celebration of Christmas that resonates with love, joy, and warmth. The decoration of banana or mango trees, gifts, music, and food - all contribute to an unforgettable Christmas celebration.

ITALY

Italy holds a unique tradition around the holiday season. The festivities center on an old woman called La Befana. She is a character from Italian folklore, known as a good witch. Every year on the eve of the Epiphany, January 5th, she takes flight. She is not like other witches you might know. She comes bearing gifts, not tricks. She flies from home to home, delivering gifts to children. Much like Santa Claus, she leaves presents for the good kids and coal for the naughty ones.

In Italian homes, families prepare for her arrival with great anticipation. This means cleaning and cooking. Italian Christmas foods are a highlight of the season. On Epiphany Eve, a special feast is cooked. Family and friends gather around the table to enjoy traditional dishes. Panettone, a sweet bread loaf from Milan, is one of the popular choices. Another favorite is torrone, a nougat-like candy made from honey, sugar, egg whites, and nuts. For drinks, Italians enjoy a glass or two of Prosecco or Asti Spumante.

Decorations are an important part of the festivities. But unlike other countries, Italy does not go overboard with lights and ornaments. You'll find simple Christmas trees and nativity scenes in most homes. The nativity scene is the main focus. Italians call it Presepe. It's a replica of the birthplace of Jesus, Bethlehem.

ITALY

Carol singing is a common practice. Carolers going door to door, singing traditional songs. The most famous Italian Christmas song is 'Tu Scendi Dalle Stelle'. It translates to 'You Come Down From The Stars'. The song talks about the birth of Jesus in a simple, humble manger.

Italy hosts some of the most famous Christmas markets. The biggest one takes place in Piazza Navona in Rome. The market dazzles with lights, decorations, and festive stalls. Vendors sell toys, candies, and Christmas ornaments. People bustle about buying gifts and enjoying the holiday spirit.

The Italians give and receive gifts twice during the holiday season. The first time is on Christmas Day, similar to most other cultures. The second time is on the eve of the Epiphany courtesy of La Befana. On this night, children hang their stockings and wait for the witch to fill them with presents.

La Befana is a fun, unique tradition in Italy. It adds a magical touch to the holiday season. Whether you embrace Santa Claus, or prefer good witches like La Befana, the joy of Christmas remains the same. It is about spreading love, goodwill, and sharing moments with loved ones.

JAMAICA

The holiday season in Jamaica is a vibrant and hearty celebration. It centers on one main event: the Grand Market. It's an all-night street market held on Christmas Eve. Vendors set up their stalls, selling a variety of goods. The air is filled with laughter, music, and a merry spirit. Kids, adults, friends, and families, all come together at the Grand Market.

Jamaican holiday foods and drinks are rich and flavorful. For Christmas dinner, many families prepare roast beef, curried goat, fried chicken, rice and peas. A standout is the Christmas pudding, also known locally as black cake. It's a rich, dark cake filled with dried fruits and spices. Rum or wine is also added to the mix. For drinks, Jamaicans enjoy the popular Sorrel. It's a sweet, yet tangy drink made from dried sorrel petals, ginger, sugar, and sometimes a bit of rum.

Santa Claus has made his way to Jamaica too. Though the temperature here may be warmer, Santa is welcomed with open arms. Children look forward to his visit, hoping to receive gifts from him. The little ones mail letters to Santa, bursting with their heart's desires. On Christmas Eve, they go to bed early, eagerly hoping for the gifts they've asked for.

JAMAICA

Decorations are a big part of the Jamaican Christmas. Houses, shops, and streets are adorned with lights. Christmas trees are decorated with baubles, stars, and tinsels. Homemade crafts also serve as decorations. Some families also put flags and balloons for a more festive look.

Music is a vital part of any celebration, and in Jamaica, it's no different. Reggae Christmas carols are a unique Jamaican twist on the tradition. Carolers travel from house to house, singing popular Jamaican Christmas songs. "Reggae Christmas" by Bryan Adams and "Santa Claus (Do You Ever Come to the Ghetto)" by Carlene Davis are among the most favorite ones.

The Grand Market takes center stage during celebrating Christmas. On Christmas Eve, streets transform into bustling markets. They are filled with an array of goods and crafts, food, toys, and clothing. Street performers liven the atmosphere with music and dance. Children run around happily, savoring sweets and treats.

The tradition of gift-giving is alive and well in Jamaica. Presents are exchanged among family and friends. For children, the anticipation of Santa Claus bringing them gifts adds to the Christmas excitement.

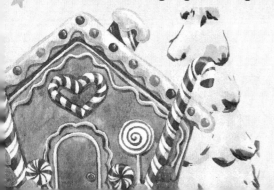

JAMAICA

Celebrating Christmas in Jamaica is about community spirit, shared merriment, and cherished traditions. The infectious positivity and warmth of the Jamaican people make it a joyful and memorable season. Yet the essence remains the same. To love, to laugh, to give, and to cherish the precious moments spent with loved ones.

JAPAN

Christmas in Japan comes with a twist. Unlike many countries, Christmas in Japan is not a religious holiday. It is a time for spreading happiness, love, and for going out on dates. Yes, that's right, Christmas Eve is popular with couples who go out for a romantic dinner. An iconic part of the season is also the unexpected tradition of having KFC dinner.

Interestingly, KFC is the Christmas food of choice for a lot of Japanese people. It started with a marketing campaign in the 1970s. "Kentucky Christmas", they called it. It was a hit. So every year, people queue up or pre-order their bucket of fried chicken. It has become so popular, even the Colonel Sanders statue outside KFC stores gets a Santa makeover.

Santa Claus, known as Santa-san in Japan, is also a part of Christmas. He is depicted the same as the western Santa - a jolly old man who brings gifts to children. However, gift giving is not as extensive as in many western cultures. Christmas gifts are usually small and simple, often exchanged between close friends or dating couples.

Decorations during Christmas are minimal yet beautiful. Christmas lights, called 'illumination' in Japan, are popular. Cities all over Japan are decorated with gorgeous light displays, bringing a magical air. Christmas trees are not that prevalent. But when they exist, they are modern and artistic.

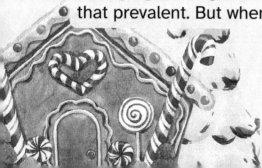

JAPAN

Christmas music is enjoyed in shopping centers and on TV. Traditional carols are played in their English versions. But Japanese pop culture also contributes to the Christmas music. Many Japanese pop and rock artists have their own Christmas songs. Those songs often top the music charts during the holiday season.

While Japan does not have a Christmas market tradition, illumination events serve a similar purpose. Streets and parks are brightly lit and people gather to enjoy the lights. In many places, small stands sell food, drinks, and local crafts.

Then comes the best part, gift giving, which is generally between close friends and romantic couples. It is not a family event as in many cultures. Many people consider it more important to present the gift in a beautiful way. So wrapping is an art, with colorful papers, ribbons, and bows.

Christmas in Japan may be different than traditional Western norms. Yet the spirit of warmth and love remains the same. It's a time for being together, sharing joy, and being happy. Regardless of where you are or how you celebrate, that's the real magic of Christmas.

LEBANON

Let's talk about Lebanon and its unique Christmas traditions. Lebanon, a country filled with cultural richness and diverse history, has vibrant Christmas celebrations. One of the most known customs involves planting seeds. People carry out a unique practice. They plant seeds in cotton wool two weeks before Christmas. They give time and care for these seeds. They grow and become part of the manger scenes.

Manger scenes, also known as Nativity scenes, have deep symbolical importance. They showcase the birth of Jesus Christ. The sprouts from the seeds carry a message of new life, growth, and hope, mirroring the essence of Christmas.

Now make way for traditional Christmas food and beverages. People in Lebanon hold festive feasts. They have a dish made of meat, rice, and a variety of spices called Kibbeh. This dish is made even more special during Christmas time. They pair it with wine spiced with cloves and nutmeg for an exotic taste. Desserts like Maamoul, a shortbread pastry with date fruit or nut fillings, take center stage.

LEBANON

Christmas is also about following customs and practices. Besides planting seeds, Lebanese people move house-to-house. They sing Arabic Christmas carols. Some of the popular ones include "Talj Talj" and "Ya Yasou."

Could you imagine Christmas without the sight of Santa Claus? In Lebanon, he is known as Father Christmas or "Baba Noel." Dressed in red, he visits homes to give presents. This tradition varies around the world. Lebanese children look forward to his arrival with a mix of excitement and joy.

Decorations provide a sense of charm and delight. Lebanese homes and streets are filled with colorful lights. Christmas trees are decorated with ornaments. The symbol of the star, representing the Star of Bethlehem, shines bright.

Singing, also known as caroling, adds to the Christmas spirit. Lebanon is no exception. People gather and sing traditional carols. They spread the message of peace, love, and joy. The sound of music fills the air.

Lebanon holds markets and festivities during this season. Stalls sell local arts, crafts, food, and drinks. The vivid display of colors is a feast to the eyes.

Gifts are part of the joyous experience. Lebanese people give and receive gifts. It takes place in homes, workplaces, and schools. It is a way to express love and good wishes.

LEBANON

Hence, Lebanon's Christmas celebrations are full of unique customs. From seed planting to Santa Claus, every aspect of the festival is filled with joy and warmth. Lebanon's Christmas traditions are a display of its rich cultural heritage.

MEXICO

Mexico has a way to warm hearts during Christmas. This beautiful country shines with joy, laughter, and colors during this season. Las Posadas, a long-loved tradition, takes center stage.

Las Posadas is a procession. It reenacts Mary and Joseph's search for shelter. It starts from the 16th of December and ends on Christmas Eve, the 24th. Each night, specific families host the Posada in their homes. A procession walks down the streets. They carry candles and sing songs. They ask for shelter in a sing-song manner. The reply comes in the same rhythm. They are granted shelter. The night ends with prayers, food, and eventually, a piñata for the children.

When it comes to food, Mexico has a rich culinary tradition. The main dish during Christmas is often pork tamales. Dishes like Bacalao, a salted fish dish, and Romeritos, a plant-based dish, are also common. Ponche Navideño, a warm fruit punch, keeps everyone toasty in the chill. Desserts like buñuelos, a type of sweet fritter, are savored too.

Santa Claus is known as "Papa Noel" in Mexico. He brings gifts to children. However, the charm of Las Posadas often takes precedent over Santa Claus.

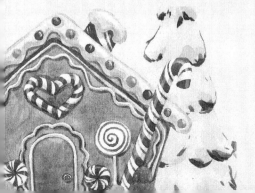

MEXICO

Christmas decorations bring warmth and color to Mexican homes and streets. Piñatas are central to Mexican Christmas decorations. These bright, star-shaped figures hang from the rooftops. They fill the hearts of the children with joy and expectations. Christmas trees, decorative lights, and nativity scenes also tell of the Christmas spirit.

Traditional Mexican Christmas music, known as "villancicos," fills the air. The lyrics of these carols tell the story of the nativity. They resonate through every home, every street corner. The sound reminds folks of the true essence of Christmas — faith, hope, and love.

The markets mirror the festive mood. Stalls sell handmade crafts, food, drinks, and other local specialties. The colors and sounds make you feel the electric atmosphere.

Mexican Christmas also includes gift-giving. Children receive gifts, not from Santa Claus, but from the Three Kings on Three King's Day, also known as Epiphany, on January 6th. On this day, children leave their shoes out filled with hay for the Kings' camels, hoping to find gifts in return.

Christmas in Mexico exhibits warmth that outrivals the winter chill. Its traditions, food, and festivities are a celebration of faith, family, and community spirit. These practices bind the people, telling a tale of joy, hope, and togetherness.

NETHERLANDS

Dutch Christmas celebrations come with a calm and modest charm. In the Netherlands, the arrival of Sinterklaas marks the beginning of the holiday season. This beloved figure arrives in mid-November with gifts and sweets, much to the delight of Dutch children.

The character of Sinterklaas is central to Dutch Christmas traditions. Unlike Santa Claus, Sinterklaas doesn't arrive from the North Pole. He comes from Spain aboard a steamboat full of presents. He is an old, wise man dressed in red, carrying a big book that knows if children have been good or bad.

Talking about food, the Dutch favor a few special treats during the holiday season. Letter-shaped chocolate initials of family members mark the breakfast table. Pepernoten, little ginger-nuts, are also enjoyed during this time. For the main feast, Dutch families gather for gourmetten, where everyone cooks their food on a table grill.

In the Netherlands, Christmas decorations are simple and natural. Houses are adorned with Christmas trees and wreaths. The use of candles is widespread, providing a warm and cozy atmosphere. In absence of a mantelpiece, shoes are placed before the fireplace or the door for Sinterklaas to leave presents in.

NETHERLANDS

Christmas music is soft and harmonious. Dutch Christmas carols known as "kerstliederen" are sung in homes and churches. Some of these are similar to English carols but are sung in the Dutch language.

As December begins, Christmas markets start appearing in Dutch towns and cities. These markets sell a wide array of items. People get to explore unique crafts, foods, and drinks. These markets provide a festive shopping experience.

Gift-giving in the Netherlands often happens on December 5th, during the Feast of Sinterklaas. This is when Sinterklaas rides over the rooftops on his white horse, dropping gifts down the chimneys for the children.

In conclusion, Christmas in the Netherlands showcases muted elegance. The arrival of Sinterklaas brings merriment and a festive mood. The celebrations maintain a simple yet heartwarming vibe. Nederlanders cherish these traditions, making every Christmas a meaningful event to remember.

PHILIPPINES

Christmas in the Philippines is a heartwarming affair. The "Simbang Gabi" or Night Mass, starts the festive spirit nine days before Christmas. The highlight, however, is the Giant Lantern Festival in San Fernando. This city is called the "Christmas Capital of the Philippines."

The Giant Lantern Festival is a sight to behold. The city of San Fernando hosts this festival just before Christmas. Every year, huge lanterns light up the night sky. These lanterns are called "parols." They symbolize the Star of Bethlehem. Making these lanterns is an art passed from generation to generation.

When it comes to food, Filipinos love to feast. They have a meal called Noche Buena after the last Simbang Gabi. This meal includes 'lechon,' a whole roasted pig, and 'bibingka,' a rice cake. 'Puto bumbong,' a purple sticky rice, is popular too. People drink a hot ginger tea named 'salabat' and a rice drink called 'kakanin.'

In the Philippines, Santa Claus is also a beloved figure. Children hang up their socks, hoping Santa will fill them with gifts. But the tradition of "Monito Monita," a gift exchange, is more common among friends, family, and co-workers.

PHILIPPINES

Christmas decorations in the Philippines are joyous and colorful. The 'parols' are the main attraction. People also decorate their homes with Christmas trees, lights, and nativity scenes, creating an atmosphere of festive cheer.

The Philippines has a rich musical heritage. Christmas carols, known as "pamamasko," are part of gatherings and celebrations. These songs and carols echo in every Filipino home.

Christmas markets in the Philippines are places of fun and frolic. Stalls sell Christmas decor, local crafts, and food. These markets add more color to the already vibrant festive spirit.

The giving of gifts is a cherished custom in the Philippines. These gifts are often exchanged on Noche Buena or the Christmas Eve dinner. The 'aguinaldo,' a gift given to children by their godparents, is a unique part of Filipino Christmas tradition.

The celebration of Christmas in the Philippines is marked by bright lights, joyful music, delicious food, and the warmth of friends and family. The Giant Lantern Festival remains the highlight, symbolizing the Filipino spirit of unity, creativity, and festive cheer.

49294044R00052